UNITED STATES BY REGION

People and Places of the
WEST
by Danielle Smith-Llera

Consultant:
Dr. David Lanegran
John S. Holl Professor of Geography
Macalester College
St. Paul, Minnesota

CAPSTONE PRESS
a capstone imprint

Fact Finders Books are published by Capstone Press,
1710 Roe Crest Drive, North Mankato, Minnesota 56003
www.mycapstone.com

Copyright © 2017 by Capstone Press, a Capstone imprint. All rights reserved. No part of this publication may be reproduced in whole or in part, or stored in a retrieval system, or transmitted in any form or by any means, electronic, mechanical, photocopying, recording, or otherwise, without written permission of the publisher.

Library of Congress Cataloging-in-Publication Data
Library of Congress Cataloging-in-Publication Data
Names: Smith-Llera, Danielle, 1971- author.
Title: People and places of the West / by Danielle Smith-Llera.
Description: North Mankato, Minnesota : Capstone Press, 2017. | Series: Fact finders. United States by region | Includes bibliographical references and index. | Audience: Grades 4 to 6.? | Audience: Ages 9 to 12.?
Identifiers: LCCN 2016010776| ISBN 9781515724414 (library binding) | ISBN 9781515724469 (pbk.) | ISBN 9781515724513 (ebook pdf)
Subjects: LCSH: West (U.S.)—Juvenile literature.
Classification: LCC F596 .S66 2017 | DDC 978—dc23
LC record available at http://lccn.loc.gov/2016010776

Editorial Credits
Angie Kaelberer, editor; Cynthia Della-Rovere, designer; Svetlana Zhurkin, media researcher; Laura Manthe, production specialist

Photo Credits
Corbis: David Stoecklein, cover (top); Courtesy Scotts Bluff National Monument, 13; Granger, NYC, 10–11; iStockphoto: Cynthia Baldauf, 22; Newscom: WENN/ZOB/CB2, 29; North Wind Picture Archives, 8–9; Shutterstock: Arina P. Habich, 25, Can Balcioglu, 21, Deymos.HR, 26–27, Everett Historical, 12, 19, Jim in SC, 18, Lee Prince, 15, Luciano Mortula, 23, Rigucci, cover (bottom), Stacey Lynn Payne, 6, topseller, 17

Design and Map Elements by Shutterstock

Table of Contents

Introduction 4
Chapter 1: History and Growth 8
Chapter 2: Land and Climate 14
Chapter 3: Jobs and Economy 20
Chapter 4: People and Culture 24

Glossary *30*
Read More *31*
Internet Sites *31*
Index *32*

Introduction

People in the West might see a cactus, mountains, forests, or even a volcano or a **glacier**. Snow may cover their cities, or they might wear short sleeves all year. They might even need to wear rain boots and sunscreen on the same day.

This huge region includes 11 states. They are Alaska, Hawaii, Washington, Oregon, Idaho, Wyoming, Montana, Colorado, California, Utah, and Nevada.

Populations of the western states vary. The West includes both of the states with the most and fewest numbers of people. The state with the most people is California and the one with the fewest is Wyoming. The others fall somewhere in between.

glacier: a large, slow-moving sheet of ice

Alaska is shown much smaller than its actual size.

The West Region by Rank

Let's see how the states in the West compare to each other. This chart includes each state and ranks it by population and area. Each state's capital and nickname are also listed. Some nicknames make sense. California is called the Golden State because many gold mines were located there. But why is Utah the Beehive State? You may have to do some research to find out the reason!

Washington state is nicknamed the Evergreen State. The area is covered with evergreen forests.

State	Population	Rank	Square Miles	Rank	Capital	Nickname
Alaska	736,732	48	656,424	1	Juneau	Last Frontier
California	38,802,500	1	163,707	3	Sacramento	Golden State
Colorado	5,355,866	22	104,100	8	Denver	Centennial State
Hawaii	1,419,561	40	6,459	47	Honolulu	Aloha State
Idaho	1,634,464	39	83,574	14	Boise	Gem State
Montana	1,023,579	44	147,046	4	Helena	Treasure State
Nevada	2,839,099	35	110,567	7	Carson City	Silver State
Oregon	3,970,239	27	98,386	9	Salem	Beaver State
Utah	2,942,902	33	84,904	13	Salt Lake City	Beehive State
Washington	7,061,530	13	71,303	18	Olympia	Evergreen State
Wyoming	584,153	51	97,818	10	Cheyenne	Equality State

Chapter 1
History and Growth

For thousands of years, the land gave western American Indian tribes all they needed to live. The Chumash settled along the Pacific coast. Paiutes, Shoshones, and Utes lived in the desert. The Nez Perce lived near rivers in present-day Washington and Idaho. Further north were the Tlingits of Alaska.

Some American Indians in the West built and lived in tepees.

Near the coast women collected nuts and berries from the forests. Men fished in the rivers and the Pacific Ocean. On the open **plains**, men hunted deer and buffalo with bows and arrows. Women cooked and preserved meat and turned hides into clothing. Some tribes lived in wooden tepee frames covered with grasses or animal skins.

> **plains:** a large, flat area of land with few trees

Europeans Arrive

In 1542 Spanish explorer Juan Rodríguez Cabrillo and his crew were the first Europeans to visit the Pacific Coast. In 1769 Spanish settlers built a military fort in what is now San Diego. The fort was the first permanent European settlement on the Pacific Coast. The Spanish also built **missions** to spread the Christian religion to the American Indians.

mission: a church or settlement where religious leaders live and work

Spanish explorers chose San Diego Bay for building a military fort.

Other explorers were interested in the West. In the 1700s Russian explorers sailed along the Pacific coast into Alaska. They traded with American Indians for sea otter furs. English and French traders set up trading posts on the Columbia River. They collected furs to trade for tea and silk from China.

Western Expansion

The U.S. government wanted to claim western lands. In 1803 President Thomas Jefferson made the Louisiana Purchase. He bought a huge piece of land from the French. It included large parts of Wyoming, Montana, and Colorado.

The United States took over more of the West in 1846. That year Great Britain and the United States signed the Oregon Treaty. The agreement set a border between the western United States and British Canada. Two years later the United States won the Mexican-American War. The United States received land that became the states of California, Nevada, and Utah, as well as parts of Colorado and Wyoming.

During the Gold Rush, some miners used a device called a sluice to collect gold.

Thousands of Americans dreamed of better lives in the West. Settlers in covered wagons made the difficult journey west on the Oregon Trail. In 1848 gold was discovered in the Sierra Nevada Mountains. Thousands of people moved west hoping to strike it rich during the Gold Rush.

The United States also spread beyond Canada and the Pacific Ocean. It bought Alaska from Russia in 1867 and added the territory of Hawaii in 1900. In 1959 Hawaii and Alaska became the last states admitted to the Union.

The Oregon Trail

The Oregon Trail began in Missouri and stretched about 2,200 miles (3,500 kilometers) to Oregon. As many as 500,000 settlers traveled it between the early 1840s and 1870. American Indian routes formed much of the trail. The trail included the South Pass, which was an easier path through the Rocky Mountains.

People traveled in covered wagons pulled by oxen. They formed wagon trains of up to 1,000 people for safety and support. The journey took between four to six months. At least 20,000 settlers died during the trip, most from diseases.

By 1870 railroad travel replaced the covered wagons. Today, parts of the trail can still be seen in areas of the West.

Chapter 2
Land and Climate

The West includes forests, deserts, and mountain ranges. The Rocky Mountains spread from Canada to New Mexico. East of the mountains are the Great Plains. They include much of Montana, Wyoming, and Colorado.

The Great Basin is a desert region that makes up most of Nevada and a large part of Utah. It also includes parts of California, Oregon, Idaho, and Wyoming. Death Valley, California, is in the Great Basin. It's the hottest and driest place in the United States. Its temperatures can reach more than 120 degrees Fahrenheit (49 degrees Celsius)! And it gets only 2 inches (5 centimeters) of rain each year.

FACT

The world's hottest temperature was recorded at Death Valley on July 10, 1913. It was 134 degrees F (57 degrees C).

Other parts of the West get lots of moisture. Hoh Rain Forest in Washington receives at least 150 inches (381 cm) of rain and snow each year. But that's nothing compared to some areas in Alaska and Hawaii. One area in Alaska averages 237 inches (602 cm) of rain and snow. Hawaii is even rainier. Its wettest place is Mount Waialeale on Kauai island. About 450 inches (1,143 cm) of rain falls on the mountain's peak every year!

Mount Waialeale in Hawaii has beautiful waterfalls that fall from the mountain. This is one of the wettest areas in the world.

Mountains, Lakes, and Rivers

North America's highest mountain range can be found in Alaska. It is called the Alaska Range. At 20,310 feet (6,190 meters), Denali is the tallest. Many large glaciers are located in the mountains.

The Sierra Nevada mountains are the home of Lake Tahoe. It's North America's largest mountain lake. In summer people swim and paddleboard in the lake. In winter they slide down mountainsides on tubes, skis, and snowboards.

Major rivers cross the West too. The Columbia flows from Canada to the Pacific Ocean in Oregon. The Colorado River begins in the Rocky Mountains of Colorado and flows southwest into Mexico.

> **FACT**
>
> No roads can cross the rugged land surrounding Alaska's Glacier Bay National Park near Juneau. The only way to see the glaciers is by boat or airplane.

At more than 2 million years old, Lake Tahoe is an ancient lake.

Natural Wonders

In California the giant **sequoia** trees amaze people. Kings Canyon National Park is home to one of the world's biggest trees. Nicknamed "General Sherman," the tree is about 275 feet (84 m) tall. It measures 25 feet (8 m) around and is more than 2,000 years old.

The hot springs and **geysers** in Wyoming's Yellowstone Park put on a great show. The famous geyser Old Faithful shoots high into the air almost every hour.

When Old Faithful erupts, the water shoots around 140 feet (42 m) into the air.

sequoia: a giant evergreen tree that grows mainly in California

geyser: an underground spring that shoots hot water and steam through a hole in the ground

In Hawaii volcanoes formed the islands. Five of Hawaii's volcanoes are still active. They are Kilauea, Mauna Loa, Hualalai, Haleakala, and Lo'ihi. Mauna Loa's last eruption was in 1984. But Kilauea has been erupting ever since 1983! Both volcanoes are part of Volcanoes National Park.

Earthquakes

Earthquakes happen when the plates that form Earth's crust shift. When the plates move, they form **fault** lines. The West is the site of several of the world's largest faults. They include the San Andreas and Hayward Faults in California and the Denali Fault System in Alaska.

Several major earthquakes have hit the region. In 1906 San Francisco, California, was heavily damaged by an earthquake and the fires that followed. About 3,000 people died. Another major earthquake hit the San Francisco area in 1989. It killed 63 people and caused $6 billion in damage.

The world's second-largest earthquake hit the Prince William Sound area in Alaska in 1964. The earthquake and the **tsunami** that followed it killed 131 people. It also destroyed much of the city of Anchorage.

fault: a crack in the earth where two plates meet; earthquakes often occur along faults

tsunami: a large, destructive wave caused by an underwater earthquake

Chapter 3

Jobs and Economy

Westerners use their region's natural resources to produce goods. Airplanes and highways move people and products in and out of the West.

Fishing, Logging, and Mining

Rivers flowing into the Pacific Ocean provide food and jobs, just as they did for the region's earliest people. Many fishers live near rivers, such as Alaska's Copper River and California's Sacramento River. Fishers catch salmon and crab in Alaska's icy waters. They fish for sardines and swordfish off the California coast and yellowfin tuna in Hawaii.

Some cities such as Seattle began as logging communities. Forests grow from Montana and Idaho down to Colorado. The northern Pacific coast has many forests too. Loggers cut down trees and plant seeds for new trees. Sawmills cut and sand the trees into boards used in construction all over the world.

The California Gold Rush lasted only a few years. But people still mine for gold and other minerals in the West. Mining companies in Alaska and California drill for oil. Tanker ships filled with oil travel from ports in Alaska and California to places all over the world.

Fishing for salmon is one of Alaska's most important industries.

Farming and Ranching

Western farmers grow many crops. More than half of the fruits, nuts, and vegetables Americans eat come from California. In Hawaii farmers grow pineapples and coffee beans. Washington orchards produce cherries, apples, and pears.

Some western states, such as Montana, have more cows than people. Cattle are raised for their meat and milk. California is the top U.S. producer of milk and other dairy products. Ranchers in Nevada and the rest of the Great Basin grow fields of hay for animal feed.

Manufacturing and Technology

Most jobs in the West don't depend on the weather or landscape. Factories build airplanes, computers, electronics, and software. Hundreds of computer companies are located in an area of northern California called the Silicon Valley. Engineers and coders design software, video games, and websites.

With more than 28,000 farms and ranches, agriculture is Montana's leading industry.

Palo Alto, California, has been a technology center since Stanford University was founded there in 1885. Stanford graduates started computer companies, such as Google and Yahoo. The social media company Facebook has its headquarters in nearby Menlo Park.

Golden Gate Bridge

The famous Golden Gate Bridge greets visitors to San Francisco, California. It was completed in 1937 to connect San Francisco and Marin County. Cables hold the 4,200-foot (1,280-m) orange steel bridge above the water.

Each day more than 100,000 vehicles cross the bridge. The bridge also has an area for people to cross on foot or by bike.

Chapter 4
People and Culture

Jobs aren't the only reason people move west. The region's climate and landscape attract new residents. People in Denver, Colorado, enjoy skiing, hiking, and mountain biking in the Rocky Mountains. In Alaska helicopters take daring skiers even higher into the mountains. In Sandpoint, Idaho, chairlifts carry people and bikes up Schweitzer Mountain. Bikers then speed down the mountain trails.

City Life

Los Angeles, California, has the largest population in the West. With 3.9 million people, it is the second largest U.S. city. Only New York City is larger. Los Angeles is the center of the American film and TV industry.

The Rocky Mountains have helped make Colorado a popular place to ski.

Westerners also enjoy nature inside their cities. Thousands of acres of parks fill Denver, Colorado, with fountains, lakes, and a zoo. Inside Portland, Oregon, trails wind through a forest. The Wilbur D. May Arboretum in Reno, Nevada, has more than 4,000 desert plants. Visitors to the Oregon Coast Aquarium in Newport watch sea lions, sea otters, seals, and other wildlife.

Many western cities are also known for their local food. People have gathered at Pike Place Market in Seattle to buy fish, herbs, and vegetables since 1907. Fresh berries, greens, and cheese are available at California's Santa Monica Farmers' Market.

Preserving Heritage

As people walk through Seattle's Pioneer Square, a huge **totem pole** reminds them of people who once lived there. American Indians carved and painted human and animal faces out of cedar to tell stories. The Totem Heritage Center in Ketchikan, Alaska, has totem poles that are more than 100 years old.

White **adobe** buildings with red clay roofs signal that much of the West was once Spanish territory. Towns such as Santa Barbara, California, preserve mission buildings built more than 250 years ago. Today California has the largest Latino population of any state. About 15 million Latinos live there.

> **totem pole:** a wooden pole carved and painted with animals, plants, and other objects that represent an American Indian tribe or family
>
> **adobe:** bricks made of clay and straw that are dried in the sun

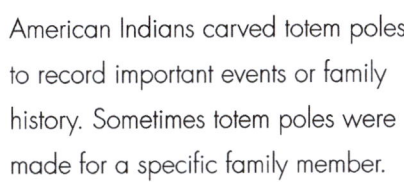

American Indians carved totem poles to record important events or family history. Sometimes totem poles were made for a specific family member.

Green-tiled roofs topped with gold dragons mark an entrance to San Francisco's Chinatown. It's the largest Chinese community outside of China. Chinese **immigrants** came to the region during the 1800s. Many business signs are written in Chinese. In an open square, people practice martial arts and play Chinese chess.

Immigrants brought their native foods with them. People slurp Chinese noodles and eat corn tortillas everywhere from Los Angeles to Honolulu. People also enjoy American Indian foods, such as fry bread and buffalo steak. In the Northwest meals include salmon and crab from nearby waters as well.

immigrant: a person who moves from one country to live permanently in another

Celebrating the West

Westerners gather to celebrate during all seasons. Each spring in Wenatchee, Washington, they twist colorful ribbons around maypoles during the Apple Blossom Festival. Summer is for tasting garlic-flavored ice cream at the Gilroy Garlic Festival in California. Visitors to the pumpkin festival in Half Moon Bay, California, eat pies and watch people carve enormous pumpkins. Daring people jump into icy water during the Winter Carnival in Whitefish, Montana.

The West is rich not only in landscapes, but also cultures. Each year 250,000 visitors gather in Seattle, Washington, to celebrate these cultures at the Northwest Folklife Festival. Dancers move to drum beats at American Indian celebrations called powwows in every western state.

FACT

The Space Needle was built for the 1962 World's Fair in Seattle. Elevators take visitors up the 605-foot (185-m) tower to look down at the city.

At the Half Moon Bay Pumpkin Festival, people show off their pumpkin-carving skills.

With its natural beauty, outdoor activities, and job opportunities, the West has long been a place where people want to visit and live. Its growth is expected to continue for years to come.

Glossary

adobe (uh-DOH-bee)—bricks made of clay and straw that are dried in the sun

fault (FAWLT)—a crack in the earth where two plates meet; earthquakes often occur along faults

geyser (GYE-zur)—an underground spring that shoots hot water and steam through a hole in the ground

glacier (GLAY-shur)—a large, slow-moving sheet of ice

immigrant (IM-uh-gruhnt)—a person who moves from one country to live permanently in another

mission (MISH-uhn)—a church or settlement where religious leaders live and work

plains (PLAYNZ)—a large, flat area of land with few trees

sequoia (suh-KWOI-uh)—a giant evergreen tree that grows mainly in California

totem pole (TOH-tuhm POLE)—a wooden pole carved and painted with animals, plants, and other objects that represent an American Indian tribe or family

tsunami (tsoo-NAH-mee)—a large, destructive wave caused by an underwater earthquake

Read More

Harvey, Dan. *Rocky Mountain: Colorado, Utah, Wyoming.* Let's Explore the States. Broomall, Pa.: Mason Crest, 2015.

Levy, Janey. *Native Peoples of the Northwest Coast.* Native Peoples of North America. New York: Gareth Stevens Publishing, 2017.

Rau, Dana Meachen. *The West.* A True Book. New York: Children's Press, 2012.

Walker, Robert. *What's in the West?* All around the U.S. New York: Crabtree Publishing Company, 2012.

Internet Sites

FactHound offers a safe, fun way to find Internet sites related to this book. All of the sites on FactHound have been researched by our staff.

Here's all you do:

Visit www.facthound.com

Type in this code: 9781515724414

Check out projects, games and lots more at
www.capstonekids.com

Index

American Indians, 8–9, 10, 11, 26

cities, 4, 20, 25
    Denver, 7, 24, 25
    Los Angeles, 24, 27
    Portland, 25
    San Francisco, 19, 23, 27
    Seattle, 20, 25, 26, 28

earthquakes, 19

farms, 22

festivals, 28

fishing, 9, 20

food, 20, 25, 27

Golden Gate Bridge, 23

Gold Rush, 13, 21

jobs, 20, 22, 24

lakes, 16, 25

land, 8, 12, 14, 22, 24, 28
    deserts, 8, 14, 25
    forests, 4, 9, 14, 15, 20, 25
    glaciers, 4, 16
    Great Basin, 14, 22
    mountains, 4, 13, 14, 15, 16, 24
    plains, 9, 14
    volcanoes, 4, 19

logging, 20

Louisiana Purchase, 12

Mexican-American War, 12

mining, 6, 21

missions, 10

Oregon Trail, 13

plants, 18, 25

population, 4, 6, 7, 24, 26

rain, 4, 14, 15

rivers, 8, 9, 11, 16, 20

technology, 22–23

temperatures, 14